SEASONS

Spring

by Mari Schuh

Kaleidoscope
Minneapolis, MN

Where the Quest for Discovery Begins

This edition first published in 2024 by Kaleidoscope Publishing, Inc.

For information regarding permission, write to

Kaleidoscope Publishing, Inc.
6012 Blue Circle Drive
Minnetonka, MN 55343

Library of Congress Control Number
2023937025

ISBN
978-1-64519-720-1 (library bound)
978-1-64519-768-3 (ebook)

Bigfoot Jr. lurks within one of the images in this book. It's up to you to find him!

Table of Contents

Spring Is Here!

Luka and Chan get ready to play outside. "What should I wear?" Luka asks.

"Spring is here, so it's getting warmer outside," Chan says. "But today is rainy. So you will want to wear a coat."

FUN FACT

Spring is a rainy season.

Spring is a season of change. In most places, the **temperature** slowly goes up.

Spring has many kinds of weather. Days can be hot or cool. They can be cloudy, sunny, or stormy.

Thunderstorms and tornadoes can happen in spring.

Earth's seasons are winter, spring, summer, and fall. Spring comes after winter.

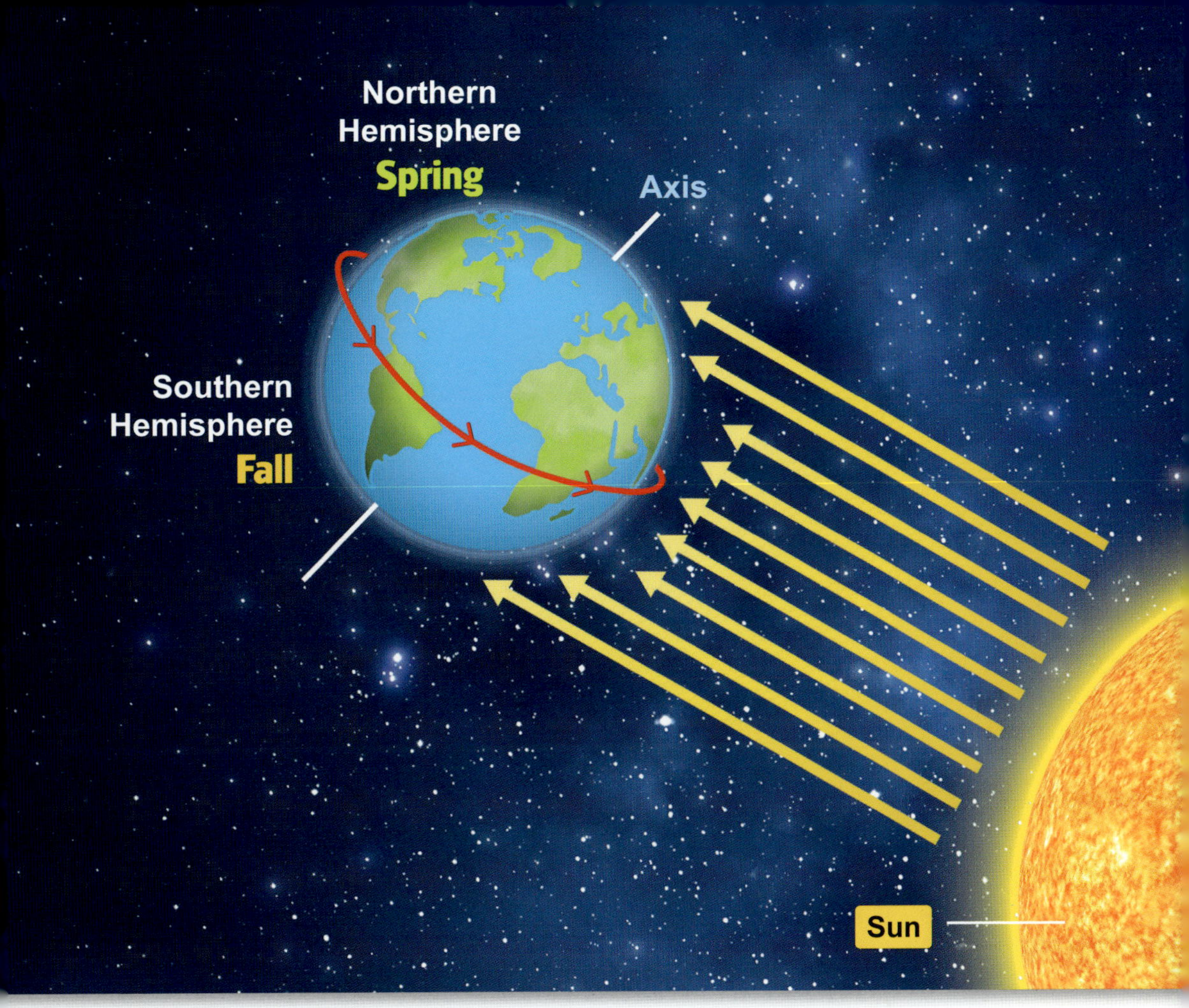

Earth **tilts** as it spins on its **axis**. As Earth travels around the Sun, some areas get more sunlight. Spring has more sunlight than winter. On Earth's northern half, spring starts in March.

Spring Is Fun!

People enjoy
spring weather.
Kids ride bikes
and climb trees.
They play hide-and-seek.

People watch baseball games. They go to festivals and concerts too.

Farmers plant **crops** in spring. People plant gardens. Sun and rain help them grow.

What Do People
Use in Spring?

What do you use in spring?

Animals Are Busy

FUN FACT
Birds build nests with twigs, leaves, and grass.

Birds are busy in spring. They build nests. They find seeds and nuts to eat.

FUN FACT
Baby ducks hatch in spring.

Loons **migrate** in spring. They fly north. Then they build nests and lay eggs.

Many loons come back to the same area every spring.

FUN FACT
Bees build their hives in spring.

Bees visit flowers. They gather nectar and pollen. They bring the food to their colony.

Arctic hares shed their winter coats. Their new fur is **camouflage**. It blends in with grass and leaves.

arctic hare with winter coat

arctic hare with spring coat

Plants in Spring

Tulips and daffodils bloom in spring.

The soil gets warmer in spring. New plants start to grow. They grow stems and leaves.

Spring is colorful! Green grass covers lawns and fields. Colorful flowers bloom.

"Today is a good day to play outside. It is so sunny!" Luka says.

"You're right, Luka. It might be cold tomorrow. The weather changes so much in spring!" Chan says.

Photo Glossary

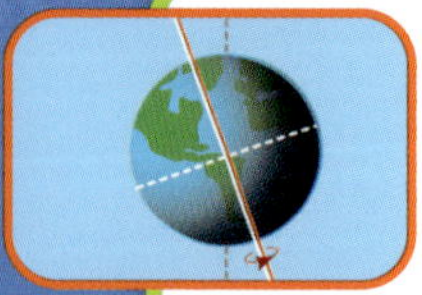

axis: An imaginary line through the center of Earth. Earth spins on its axis. One spin is one day.

camouflage: Colors and patterns that help animals blend in with their surroundings. Camouflage helps animals stay safe from enemies.

crops: Plants grown for food. Farmers plant crops such as corn and beans in spring.

migrate: To move regularly to another area at a particular time of year. Some animals migrate to warmer areas every spring.

temperature: The measure of how hot or cold something is. A thermometer measures temperature.

thunderstorms: Heavy rainstorms with lightning and thunder. Thunderstorms usually have thick clouds and strong winds.

tilts: Leans, tips, or slants to one side. Earth tilts on its axis.

tornadoes: Powerful whirling winds. Tornadoes are shaped like funnels.

Read More

Earley, Christina. *In the Spring.* New York, NY: Crabtree Publishing, 2023.

Leaf, Christina. *Spring.* Minneapolis, MN: Bellwether Media, 2023.

Press, J.P. *Spring Weather.* Minneapolis, MN: Bearport Publishing, 2022.

Youssef, Jagger. *Seasons.* New York, NY: PowerKids Press, 2023.

Websites

FACTSURFER

Factsurfer.com gives you a safe, fun way to find more information.

1. Go to www.factsurfer.com.
2. Enter "Spring" into the search box and click 🔍
3. Select your book cover to see a list of related websites.

About the Author

Mari Schuh's love of reading began with cereal boxes at the kitchen table. Today she is the author of hundreds of nonfiction books for beginning readers. Mari lives in the Midwest with her husband and their sassy house rabbit. Learn more about her at marischuh.com.

INDEX

PHOTO CREDITS

The images in this book are reproduced through the courtesy of: stable/Shutterstock Images, cover (top left); fotohunter/Shutterstock Images, cover (top right); EyesTravelling/Shutterstock Images, cover (bottom); domnitsky/Shutterstock Images, title page; Tiger Images/Shutterstock Images, p. 3; TORWAISTUDIO/Shutterstock Images, p. 4–5; Nadzeya Pakhomava/Shutterstock Images, p. 6; Tomas Ragina/Shutterstock Images, p. 6 (thermometer); muratart/Shutterstock Images, p. 7 (top); Rasica/Shutterstock Images, p. 7 (bottom); Smileus/Shutterstock Images, p. 8 (circle); Mihai_Andritoiu/Shutterstock Images, p. 8 (all four seasons); Sergey Novikov/Shutterstock Images, p. 10; Purino/Shutterstock Images, p. 10 (circle); meolia/Shutterstock Images, p. 11; oticki/Shutterstock Images, p. 12; Singkham/Shutterstock Images, p. 12 (circle); Marco La Melia/Shutterstock Images, p. 13 (kite); eurobanks/Shutterstock Images, p. 13 (birdhouse); tale/Shutterstock Images, p. 13 (rain boots and umbrella); FocusStocker/Shutterstock Images, p. 13 (soccer ball); Cory Woodruff/Shutterstock Images, p. 13 (sunglasses); Svitlana Martynova/Shutterstock Images, p. 13 (easter basket); bangchuck/Shutterstock Images, p. 13 (hoodie); Pixel-Shot/Shutterstock Images, p. 13 (gardening tools); Rob Jansen/Shutterstock Images, p. 14; Sergii Figurnyi/Shutterstock Images, p. 15 (top); PeilunZ/Shutterstock Images, p. 15 (bottom); schankz/Shutterstock Images, p. 16; FotoRequest/Shutterstock Images, p. 17; anastasia buinovska/Shutterstock Images, p. 18 (spring flowers); Alexander Raths/Shutterstock Images, p. 18–19; MEE KO DONG/Shutterstock Images, p. 19; Sergey Novikov/Shutterstock Images, p. 20; Sergey Novikov/Shutterstock Images, p. 21; FotoRequest/Shutterstock Images, p. 22 (camouflage); Tomas Ragina/Shutterstock Images, p. 22 (temperature); Rasica/Shutterstock Images, p. 22 (tornadoes); Jim Cumming/Shutterstock Images, p. 22 (migrate); Alchemist from India/Shutterstock Images, p. 22 (crops); muratart/Shutterstock Images, p. 22 (thunderstorm); Tsekhmister/Shutterstock Images, p. 23.